# The A
# Ocean



by William Johns

## Table of Contents

Chapter 1

# What Is an Ocean?

An ocean is very big. It is a vast area of salty water.

The four oceans cover more than half of Earth. Each ocean has a name. Can you find the ocean closest to you?

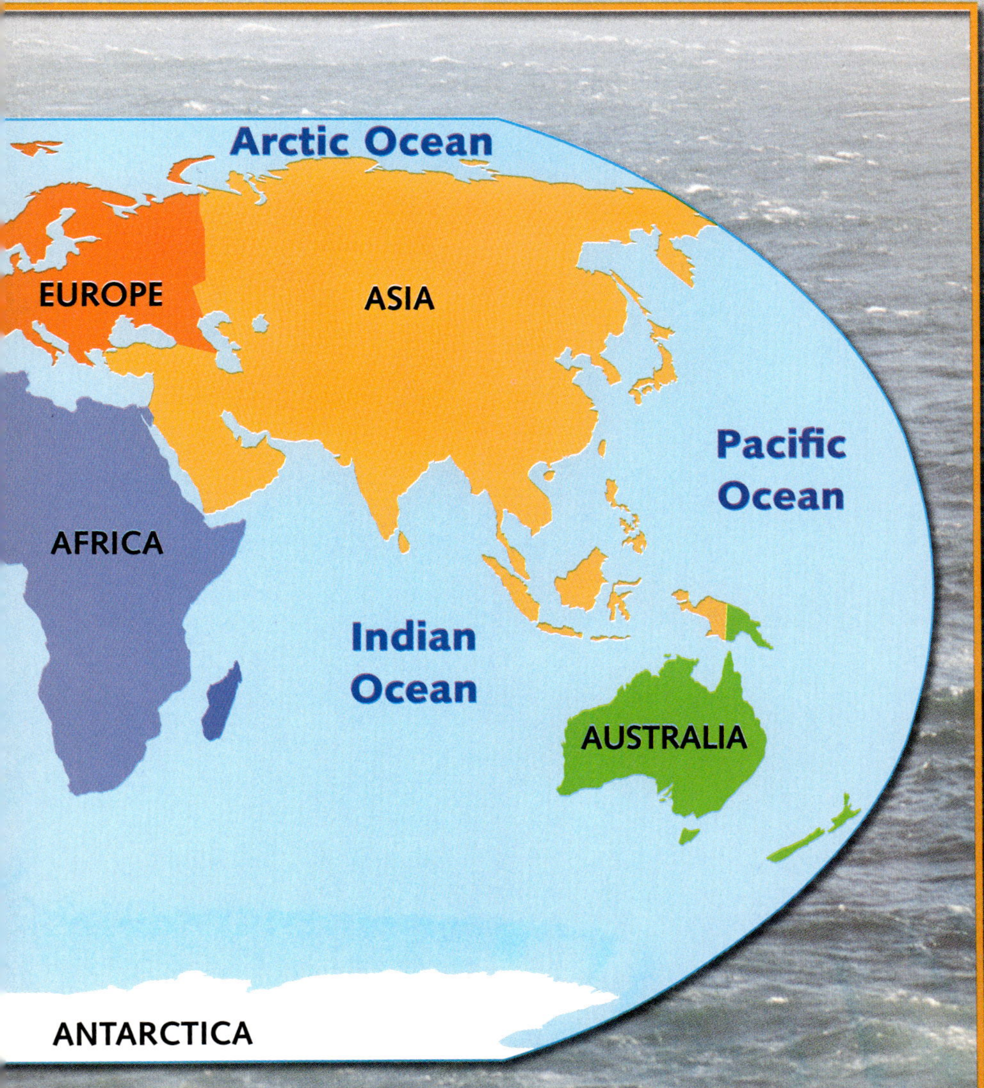

Chapter 2

# What Lives in the Ocean?

There is an amazing world in the ocean. Plants big and small live there.

Kelp

Coral looks like a plant. But it is a group of animals. All kinds of animals live in the ocean.

Coral

Chapter 3

# What Has Fins?

Fish have fins. Millions of fish live in the ocean. A fish has a body built for life in the sea. A fish has gills so that it can breathe under the water. A fish uses its fins to swim.

Reef Shark

Fish come in all sizes. There are little fish. There are big fish, too. When fish swim in a group it is called a school of fish.

Butterfly Fish

Anthias Fish

Fish can be any color. Can you find the purple fish? Can you find the yellow fish?

Fish can have patterns.
What patterns do you see?

Smallmouth Grunts

Butterfly Fish

Puffer Fish

Swordfish

**Flounder**

Fish can be all kinds of shapes. They can be long and thin. They can be round. They can be flat!

Whales look like fish. But whales are not fish. Whales have fins, but they do not have gills. Whales need air to breathe. They swim to the top of the water to get air.

Look! The baby whale is swimming with its mother. It will stay with its mother until it is about a year old.

Chapter 4

# What Has Legs? What Has Arms?

Crabs have eight legs and two claws. A crab is an ocean animal that has a shell. Crabs can walk on land.

Sea stars have five arms. A sea star is also called a star fish. But a sea star is not a fish. If a sea star loses an arm the arm will grow back!

The ocean is an amazing world. It is a wonderful mix of plants and animals big and small!